GIFTS OF LOVE

GIFTS OF
LOVE

NEW HYMNS FOR
TODAY'S WORSHIP

Carolyn Winfrey Gillette

GENEVA PRESS
Louisville, Kentucky

Book design by Running Feet Books

First edition
Published by Geneva Press
Louisville, Kentucky

This book is printed on acid-free paper that meets the American National Standards Institute Z39.48 standard. ∞

Printed in the United States of America

00 01 02 03 04 05 06 07 08 09 — 10 9 8 7 6 5 4 3 2 1

Library of Congress Cataloging-in-Publication Data

A catalog record for this book is available from the Library of Congress.
ISBN 0-664-50134-6

Contents

THE CHURCH IN THE WORLD

Preface

We often learn the Christian faith through music. Much of what we understand about God, the church, the world, and ourselves is learned through Sunday school music and vacation Bible school songs, through singing in church youth choirs and at summer church camps, and through the hymns of the church. In times of great joy or challenge, reflection and recommitment, awe and emotion, we find ourselves remembering and singing the music of the church.

In 1998 I attended the Synod of the Trinity's Synod School at Wilson College (a Presbyterian-related college in Chambersburg, Pennsylvania). A teacher in a class on the Psalms mentioned that people often remember things set to music and that someone had once written the Ten Commandments as a hymn, but no one knew that hymn. I decided to write a hymn to help my three children learn the Ten Commandments. That was the beginning of an exciting year of writing hymns, sharing them with others (often by way of the Internet), and learning from other hymn writers who have helped me along the way. The many kind notes and worship bulletins from new friends on the Internet who have sung the hymns in their churches have been a source of amazement and joy.

I have chosen to write these new hymn texts to familiar tunes and have listed alternate hymn tunes where possible. Hymn numbers are given for tunes in *The Hymnal 1982* (HY, Episcopal), the *Lutheran Book of Worship* (LBW, 1978), *The New Century Hymnal* (NCH, United Church of Christ, 1995), *The Presbyterian Hymnal* (PH, 1990), and *The United Methodist Hymnal* (UMH, 1989). I hope that these new words will help congregations to reflect on their faith in new ways and make connections between the Christian faith and contemporary life.

Some of the people who helped me write this book began the process of helping me many years ago. My parents, David and Jane Winfrey, surrounded me with faith and love when I was first learning what it means to be a Christian. Washington Square United Methodist Church and Otterbein United Methodist Church nurtured my love for church music and gave living examples of people filled with the love of Christ. College and seminary professors, and Presbyterian churches I served in Andover and Hamburg, New Jersey, helped me grow in my understanding of faith and ministry, as found in these hymns. David Carlisle, a pastor and friend, read my first hymn at Synod School and suggested that *Gifts of Love* would be a good title for my first book of hymns. Ruth Duck, a talented hymn writer and seminary professor, offered suggestions and encouragement early on. John Dallas, another gifted hymn writer and pastor, kindly critiqued this collection of hymns and encouraged me as well. Robert Bullock, editor of *The Presbyterian Outlook*, was very supportive, publishing many of the hymns in that national magazine. The participants at a Presbyterian Writers Guild hymn writing workshop at Union Theological Seminary, Richmond, helped me grow in hymn writing. Ronda Hughes, a national staff person for Church World Service, has enthusiastically shared my hymns with many other churches. Jerry and Louise Gillette, my in-laws, were among the first to hear these hymns; they have encouraged me to keep writing. Members of the First Presbyterian Church in Pitman, New Jersey, the congregation that I am serving as co-pastor, have joyfully sung many of these hymns during this past year. Thomas G. Long, director of Geneva Press, has been a very helpful friend as well as editor.

I especially thank my husband Bruce for his love, encouragement, and many helpful suggestions for hymn topics and improvements, and for his sharing of my hymns with others. We are co-pastors, and this process of writing, refining, and sharing hymns has been another way we have been able to share in ministry together. And I want to thank John, Catherine, and Sarah, our children, who are the reasons I started writing these new texts. They have willingly listened to many of the hymns and joined in singing some of them, and so they have encouraged me to pass along my faith, through music, to a new generation. In the end, my prayer is that the one who is the ultimate inspiration for these hymns, our loving God, will be glorified by them.

GIFTS OF LOVE

1 Your Word Is Like a Lamp, O Lord

CANONBURY   LM

Your word is like a lamp, O Lord,
And like a light to guide our way;
For in this ever-changing world
It bears your promise every day.

You showed your love to Israel,
And to the world you sent your Son—
A witness without parallel;
The scriptures tell what you have done.

You speak your word in history,
To cultures bound by time and place.
Yet in the Bible we can see
The boundless reaching of your grace.

God, open wide each heart and mind
By your own Spirit now, we pray,
That in your scriptures we may find
New strength to serve you every day.

TUNE: Robert Schumann, 1829 ("Lord, Speak to Me That I May
    Speak," LBW 403, NCH 531, PH 426, UMH 463)
ALTERNATE TUNE: MARYTON ("O Master, Let Me Walk with
    Thee," HY 660, LBW 492, NCH 503, PH 357, UMH 430)
TEXT: Copyright © 1999 by Carolyn Winfrey Gillette. All rights
    reserved.

2 God Made the Heavens and the Earth

SOLID ROCK   LM with refrain

God made the heavens and the earth.
God's Spirit moved; they came to be.
For when God spoke, there was the light,
And solid ground, and rolling sea.

> *Refrain*
> Lord, all your world's a precious gift.
> You give dominion! Help us share
> In your creation's loving care.

God saw the earth was very good.
God spoke, and life came bursting forth:
The bright green grass, the shaded wood,
And wondrous creatures 'round the earth.

> *Refrain*

And soon it was, God spoke again:
In God's good image we were made,
To fill the earth, and tenderly
To tend the land, and love, and pray.

> *Refrain*

When I look up and see the stars,
Creation shouts your praise anew.
I humbly ask, "Lord, who am I?"
Yet we are called to work with you.

Refrain

TUNE: William Batchelder Bradbury, 1863 ("My Hope Is Built on
 Nothing Less," LBW 293, NCH 403, PH 379, UMH 368)
TEXT: Copyright © 1998 by Carolyn Winfrey Gillette. All rights
 reserved.

3 Long Ago, God Reached in Love

JESUS LOVES ME   7.7.7.7 with refrain

Long ago, God reached in love,
Sending Noah back a dove,
Promising a world made dry,
With a rainbow in the sky.

Refrain
God, you are faithful,
God, you are faithful,
God, you are faithful:
Your covenant is love!

Abraham and Sarah heard
God's surprising, joyful word:
God would give them land and more:
Children they had long hoped for.

Refrain

Ten Commandments were the way
God called people to obey,
For God wanted us to see:
In obeying, we are free.

Refrain

Jeremiah came to know
God would help us change and grow;
So God's law would fill each heart,
Giving us a fresh, new start.

Refrain
Jesus came to show the way
We can have new life today;
God fulfilled that loving plan,
Made for us when life began.

Refrain

TUNE: William Batchelder Bradbury, 1861 ("Jesus Loves Me!"
    NCH 327, PH 304, UMH 191)

4 Spirit of God

O QUANTA QUALIA   11.11.11.11

Spirit of God, you moved over the waters
Whisp'ring God's love to the whole of creation.
You breathe your life into God's sons and daughters,
Giving us talents and your inspiration.

Spirit of God, by the prophets you sought us,
Calling us back from our pride-filled behavior.
Through chosen leaders you reached us and taught us;
By your own gift we were given our Savior.

Spirit of God, like a dove you once rested,
Showing God's joy on the day Christ was baptized.
You sent Christ out to the hills to be tested,
Through you, he called us to see God with new eyes.

Spirit of God, like a mighty wind blowing:
Suddenly Christians stopped hiding and fearing.
You gave them courage and love overflowing,
So they proclaimed you to all in their hearing.

Help us to see you, still calling and caring,
Help us to know you among us, creating.
Spirit of God, give us courage and daring—
To share God's love with a world that is waiting.

TUNE: Paris *Antiphoner*, 1681. As in La Feillée's *Méthode du plain-chant*, 1808 ("God of Compassion, in Mercy Befriend Us," HY 623, LBW 337, NCH 385, PH 261, UMH 727)

TEXT: Copyright © 1999 by Carolyn Winfrey Gillette. All rights reserved.

5 God of the Women

SLANE   10.10.10.10

God of the women who answered your call,
Trusting your promises, giving their all —
Women like Sarah and Hannah and Ruth:
Give us their courage to live in your truth.

God of the women who walked Jesus' Way,
Giving their resources, learning to pray —
Mary, Joanna, Susanna, and more:
May we give freely as they did before.

God of the women long put to the test,
Left out of stories, forgotten, oppressed,
Quietly asking: "Who smiled at my birth?"
In Jesus' dying, you show us our worth.

God of the women who ran from the tomb,
Prayed with the others in that upper room,
Then felt your Spirit on Pentecost Day:
May we so gladly proclaim you today.

O God of Phoebe and ministers all,
May we be joyful in answering your call.
Give us the strength of your Spirit so near
That we may share in your ministry here.

TUNE: Irish ballad ("Be Thou My Vision," HY 488, LBW 469,
   NCH 451, PH 339, UMH 451)

6   Gifts of Love

I WANT TO BE A CHRISTIAN   Irregular

Gifts of love our Lord has given, Words of life: "I'm your
    God!
I have brought you out of Egypt; now I call.
Listen here, listen well:
When you live in gratitude, you'll keep my law.

"Have no others gods before me," says the Lord God Most
    High.
"Don't choose idols that you worship in God's place.
Know God's name, use it well.
Keep the Sabbath, for it is God's gift of grace.

"Honor father, honor mother, and rejoice! God will bless
    you.
Take no life, for God loves every child on earth.
Celebrate gifts of love;
Take to heart what marriage promises are worth.

"Do not steal from one another, nor speak lies, hurting
    others;
Do not wish for what your neighbor has, in greed."
Ten great Words, gifts from God,
Help us live in thanks for all we have received.

TUNE: African American spiritual ("Lord, I Want to Be a Christian,"
    NCH 454, PH 372, UMH 402)

7 Sing Out! Sound the Trumpets! Proclaim Jubilee!

TO GOD BE THE GLORY   11.11.11.11 with refrain

Sing out! Sound the trumpets! Proclaim jubilee!
Through words from Isaiah, we came to be free;
For, blessed by the Spirit, Christ read from that scroll,
Proclaiming his mission: to make our lives whole.

Refrain
Hear the word! Sing it out! It's good news to the poor!
Christ has come! Let us shout! We are captive no more!
Lost sight is restored, and God's world is set free:
Christ came to our world to proclaim jubilee.

But still, women struggle for lives free and fair,
And children are hungry, and loved ones despair.
Still, those long-oppressed or in prisons of fear
Are longing to call this their jubilee year.

Refrain

O God, through your Christ you knelt down to the earth,
And by your own Spirit, you give us new birth.
May we as your church have a passion to share
Your jubilee love with the world everywhere.

Refrain

TUNE: William Howard Doane, 1875 ("To God Be the Glory," PH 485,
   UMH 98)
TEXT: Copyright © 1998 by Carolyn Winfrey Gillette. All rights
   reserved.

8 Blessed Are
the Poor Among You

PROMISES   11.11.11.9 with refrain

Blessed are the poor among you, Jesus said.
Blessed are you hungry ones who long for bread.
Blessed are you mournful when your tears abound.
God is turning everything around.
Hear the good news!
God is giving you the kingdom and the laughter.
God will fill you—
And you will know the joy that overflows.

Blessed are you weary who are long oppressed,
All because you follow God in faithfulness.
Leap for joy, for God will give you life anew.
Long ago, the prophets struggled, too!
Hear the good news!
God is giving you the kingdom and the laughter.
God will fill you—
And you will know the joy that overflows.

Woe to all you rich who live with blinders on,
Feasting at your tables till the food is gone.
Woe to you who laugh and live without a care;
Woe! when people praise you everywhere.
God has spoken:
You have all received your joy and consolation.
I was hungry—
But did you share what God had given you?

God, your way of working is a great surprise!
Help us all to see your world through faithful eyes.
Only in your kingdom is our true joy found.
By your Spirit, turn our lives around!
Yours is good news!
You have offered us the kingdom and the laughter.
Please, God, fill us,
And we will know the joy that overflows.

TUNE: R. Kelso Carter, 1886 ("Standing on the Promises," UMH 374)
TEXT: Copyright © 1998 by Carolyn Winfrey Gillette. All rights
    reserved.

9   In Cana at a Wedding Feast

ELLACOMBE   CMD

In Cana at a wedding feast,
Christ worked his first great sign.
There Jesus' mother told her son,
"They don't have any wine!"
He called for six stone water jars;
They filled them to the brim;
When water changed to wine that day,
His friends believed in him.

Far from the town, the crowds pressed in
On Jesus' prayer retreat.
He healed their sick, then told his own,
"You give them food to eat!"
Five loaves of bread and two small fish
Were all they found to share,
Yet thousands ate the meal he blessed,
With baskets left to spare.

Out on the sea, the winds were strong;
The stormy waves were high;
There Jesus' friends were filled with fear
When he came walking by.
"Take heart, for it is I!" he said,
And helping Peter stand,
He calmed the storm and stirred their hearts;
God's world was in his hand.

The blind, the poor, the outcast too,
Found Christ to be their friend.
"Have mercy!" Bartimaeus said.
"I want to see again."
With great compassion and with grace,
Christ gave him back his sight.
Through deeds of power, deeds of love,
He filled our world with light.

O Lord, we see your wondrous signs
And know through faith-filled eyes:
You are new wine that brings us joy,
True bread that satisfies.
You give clear vision to your church,
You make the wounded whole.
You give us hope when seas are rough;
For you are in control!

TUNE: *Gesangbuch der Herzogl. Wirtembergischen Katholischen Hofkapelle*, 1784; alt. 1868 ("I Sing the Mighty Power of God," HY 210, LBW 251, NCH 12, PH 288, UMH 203)
TEXT: Copyright © 1999 by Carolyn Winfrey Gillette. All rights reserved.

10 God's Great Love Is So Amazing!

CONVERSE 8.7.8.7 D

God's great love is so amazing!
See—a shepherd with his flocks!
Ninety-nine are safely grazing;
One is lost among the rocks.
That good shepherd goes and searches
Till he finds the one astray.
So God says to fill our churches
With the ones who've lost their way.

God in love is always seeking!
See—a woman with her broom!
For a single coin she's sweeping
Every corner of the room.
When it's found she calls each neighbor,
Telling friends from all around.
So God says to search and labor
Till God's precious ones are found.

God keeps waiting, searching, yearning!
See—a father's heartfelt joy!
Thankful for his son's returning,
He runs out to greet his boy.
To the angry older brother,
Hear the father's patient call.
So God says to love each other,
For in Christ God loves us all.

TUNE: Charles Crozat Converse, 1868 ("What a Friend We Have in Jesus," LBW 439, NCH 506, PH 403, UMH 526)
TEXT: Copyright © 1999 by Carolyn Winfrey Gillette. All rights reserved.

THE BIBLE: SINGING THE STORY

11 When You Are Praying

AMAZING GRACE   CM

"When you are praying," Jesus said,
"Don't put on vain displays—
But close your door and speak your heart
And humbly offer praise."

Our Father in the heavenly realm,
Our Abba, ever near—
Your name is holy, set apart;
O bring your kingdom here!

God, give us all we daily need
And we will be content;
Forgive our sins as we forgive
The wrongs that we resent.

God, give us grace to follow you;
Protect us on your Way.
When evil tempts us from your path,
Deliver us, we pray.

O Lord, we turn in trust to you;
You know the things we need—
And like a parent, so you love:
The ones who ask receive.

TUNE: *Virginia Harmony*, 1831. Arr. Edwin O. Excell, 1900 ("Amazing
    Grace," HY 671, LBW 448, NCH 547, PH 280, UMH 378)
ALTERNATE TUNE: CRIMOND ("The Lord's My Shepherd,"
    HY 663, NCH 468, PH 170, UMH 136)
TEXT: Copyright © 1998 by Carolyn Winfrey Gillette. All rights
    reserved.

12 Mary Heard the Angel's Message

HYFRYDOL   8.7.8.7 D

Mary heard the angel's message:
"Greetings, Mary, favored one!
Do not fear, for God is with you;
You will one day bear God's Son."
Filled with questions, filled with wonder,
She proclaimed her faith in God:
"May it be as you have spoken;
I'm the servant of the Lord!"

When she heard her cousin's greeting,
Mary's heart was filled with joy,
So she sang of God's great blessing
Promised in her baby boy:
"God has looked on me with favor,
So I sing this song of praise.
God has worked, the proud to scatter;
Humble, hungry ones to raise."

Mary heard the shepherds' story,
Words she treasured with delight.
Then an angel gave the warning:
"Flee with Jesus in the night!"
Mary wondered in her anguish,
What would be the pain he'd know?
Fleeing then, she held him closely.
One day she would let him go.

Mary heard, "Who is my mother?
Who is in my family?
All who do my Father's bidding—
All these ones belong to me."
Later, on the hill she heard him,
"Woman, see your new son there!
You, my friend, behold your mother!"
So Christ formed new bonds of care.

When they learned the Lord had risen,
Christ's disciples met to pray.
Mary was among the faithful,
Bound in love, on Jesus' Way.
God, we see her, Christ's disciple,
Loving, learning, serving, too.
Like her, may we hear and answer,
"We, your servants, live for you."

TUNE: Rowland Hugh Prichard, 1831 ("Alleluia! Sing to Jesus!"
    HY 460, LBW 158, NCH 257, PH 144, UMH 196)
ALTERNATE TUNE: BEECHER ("Love Divine, All Loves Excelling,"
    HY 470, NCH 43, PH 343, UMH 384)

13   I Believe

AUSTRIAN HYMN   8.7.8.7 D

I believe in God the Father,
The Almighty God above,
Maker of the earth and heaven
Which were formed in God's great love—
And in Jesus, loving Jesus,
God's own Son, who makes us new.
This, the creed of generations,
Is the faith for our church, too.

Jesus, by God's Holy Spirit,
Was so wondrously conceived,
Born unto the Virgin Mary,
Who your promises believed.
Jesus, suffering under Pilate,
On a cross was crucified.
Soldiers mocked him, friends denied him;
He hung there until he died.

So it was, our Lord was buried,
In a borrowed tomb he lay.
To the dead he then descended,
Where was joy on earth that day?
There is more to God's great story:
In three days he rose again.
He ascended into heaven,
And he sits at God's right hand.

I believe what God has promised:
Christ will come as he has said.
He will judge the nations' peoples,
Both the living and the dead.
I believe God's Holy Spirit
Makes the church one family.
We're surrounded by God's people,
Saints who in our Lord believe.

I believe that God forgives us
For the times we turn away,
And that God will raise our bodies
On that resurrection day.
We rejoice we'll live forever,
Singing praise to God's great name.
This, the creed of generations,
Is the faith that we proclaim.

The Apostles' Creed
TUNE: Franz Joseph Haydn, 1797 ("Glorious Things of Thee Are
    Spoken," HY 522, LBW 358, NCH 307, PH 446, UMH 731)
TEXT: Copyright © 1998 by Carolyn Winfrey Gillette. All rights
    reserved.

14 Our God, We Are a Church Reformed

AZMON   CM

Our God, we are a church reformed,
A church reforming still:
We long to grow in your true Word,
And follow more your will.

How awesome is your sovereign rule;
You reign from heav'n above.
Yet you knelt down in Jesus Christ,
In sacrificial love.

In love, you bring your people here
And call your church to you,
That we may know salvation's joy
And serve in all we do.

You call us to community;
By faith our hearts are stirred.
In church, we seek an ordered life,
According to your Word.

As faithful stewards we find joy;
We need no rich display.
Lord, teach us all to use with care
The gifts you give each day.

The world makes gods of lesser things,
And wrongly uses power;
So by your Spirit may we work
For justice every hour.

Presbyterian Church (U.S.A.) *Book of Order* G-2.0500
TUNE: Carl Gotthelf Gläser, 1828. Arr. Lowell Mason, 1839 ("O For a
    Thousand Tongues to Sing," HY 493, LBW 559, NCH 42, PH 466,
    UMH 57)

15 Welcoming God

ASSURANCE   9.10.9.9 with refrain

Children are welcome, Christ said one day,
When the disciples just urged them away.
Children are welcome at Jesus' knee:
God's own examples for ministry.
Welcoming God, you open the Way;
Even the smallest worship and pray,
Singing with faith and serving you well,
Your life to know and good news to tell.

Women are welcome, as are the men;
Through God's own Spirit, we're partners again.
Partners as prophets, ministers, too:
No more divided—made one in you.
Welcoming God, you open the way;
Those once divided join now to pray,
Serving at Table, preaching your Word,
So that your love for all will be heard.

Outcasts are welcome; sinners are, too,
Eating with Jesus and being made new:
Some like Zacchaeus turned right around;
Wounded and poor ones felt peace profound.
God of great love, you stand at the door,
Welcoming people outcast and poor.
So you forgive and call us to be
Filled with the joy of your jubilee.

So may we welcome into our pew
All who in Jesus are being made new—
All those who seek him, wanting to know,
Wanting to love him, wanting to grow.
Welcoming God, you stand at our door,
As someone different, outcast or poor.
With longing eyes, Lord Jesus, you search.
May we all welcome you in your church.

TUNE: Phoebe Palmer Knapp, 1873 ("Blessed Assurance, Jesus Is
    Mine!" NCH 473, PH 341, UMH 369)
TEXT: Copyright © 1998 by Carolyn Winfrey Gillette. All rights
    reserved.

16　God of Generations

NICAEA　12.13.12.10

God of generations, we are all your children;
To your church we bring our gifts, our worship and our
　　song.
Young and old we follow, hand in hand together:
In your great love, together we are strong.

Christ, you welcomed children, called us to be like them,
And received a boy's small gift to feed a hungry crowd.
In our church's children, may we see you working:
More than "our future"! They are faithful now.

Spirit, freely moving, giving youth a vision,
By your grace young Jeremiah heard your loving call;
Mary was a young one when she learned her mission:
Through faithful youth, you offer truth to all.

God of men and women, Helper on our journey,
You have called us in our faith to grow and to mature.
May we keep on learning, worshiping, and praying,
That each new day, we'll serve you all the more.

Abraham and Sarah trusted in your promise:
Age was no condition when you gave them work to do.
Old and young, we follow, hand in hand together;
At every age, Lord, we belong to you.

TUNE: John Bacchus Dykes, 1861 ("Holy, Holy, Holy! Lord God
　　Almighty!" HY 362, LBW 165, NCH 277, PH 138, UMH 64)
TEXT: Copyright © 1998 by Carolyn Winfrey Gillette. All rights
　　reserved.

THE CHURCH: GOD'S LOVING COMMUNITY

17 Hear My Prayer for Unity

ABERYSTWYTH   7.7.7.7 D

"Hear my prayer for unity,"
Jesus prayed for all his own.
"May these ones you've given me
Live the love that I have shown.
Mine are yours and yours are mine;
In them I am glorified!
Now I send them as a sign;
So may they be unified."

God, we live in great discord,
Torn by issues we hold dear;
Even as we call you Lord,
We still cling to pride and fear.
Bound together, we'd be free;
We could join in serving you!
For the best theology
Starts when love makes all things new.

By your Spirit, make us one;
So the world will come to know
All the love of Christ the Son,
All your joys that overflow.
Help us put aside our strife;
Give your church a humble mind!
Christ, the Way, the Truth, the Life,
Strengthen now the ties that bind.

TUNE: Joseph Parry, 1879 ("Jesus, Lover of My Soul," HY 699, LBW 91,
    NCH 103, PH 303, UMH 479)
TEXT: Copyright © 1999 by Carolyn Winfrey Gillette. All rights
    reserved.

THE CHURCH: GOD'S LOVING COMMUNITY

18 We Thank You, God, for Teachers

A Hymn for Christian Education

WIE LIEBLICH IST DER MAIEN   7.6.7.6. D

We thank you, God, for teachers
Who help us learn your Way,
Who show by their example
How we can serve and pray,
Who find great joy in worship,
Who listen with concern;
For in their loving witness,
They help us want to learn.

We thank you, God, for children
And older people, too,
Who value times of learning
And want to grow in you,
Who seek your precious kingdom
And wisdom from above;
For wise ones of all ages
Still seek to learn your love.

We thank you, God, for families
Of every kind and size,
Who keep the vows they spoke when
Their children were baptized,
Who pray and read the Bible,
Who love and serve the poor;
They teach, by what they value,
The way of Christ our Lord.

We thank you, God, for churches
That welcome one and all,
That nurture every person
In answer to Christ's call.
So fill us with your Spirit,
And give us life anew,
That we may help each other
Live faithfully in you.

TUNE: Johann Steurlein, 1575 ("We Come as Guests Invited,"
   LBW 412, PH 517)
ALTERNATE TUNE: ELLACOMBE ("I Sing the Mighty Power of
   God," HY 210, LBW 251, NCH 12, PH 288, UMH 203)
TEXT: Copyright © 1999 by Carolyn Winfrey Gillette. All rights
   reserved.

19   O God, in Your Love

ST. DENIO   11.11.11.11

O God, in your love, you have made us unique:
In gifts and traditions, in service we seek,
In race and in culture and family design —
Diverse are the branches in Jesus the Vine.

Lord Jesus, you came to bring God's love on earth;
You welcomed the outcasts and showed us our worth.
You reached out to people whom others despised —
You said all are precious in God's loving eyes.

O Christ, with your welcome your church feels unease:
We stand at closed doors tightly holding the keys.
Yet this is your body, the church that you love —
O Lord, do you weep for your church from above?

So may your church welcome in loving accord
All people who want to serve Jesus our Lord.
O Spirit, unite us in Jesus the Son —
In mission and ministry, God, make us one.

TUNE: Welsh folk hymn, adapted in *Caniadau y Cyssegr*, 1839
("Immortal, Invisible, God Only Wise," HY 423, LBW 526, NCH 1,
PH 263, UMH 103)
TEXT: Copyright © 1998 by Carolyn Winfrey Gillette. All rights
reserved.

20 There Is a Mighty Question

ANGEL'S STORY   7.6.7.6 D

There is a mighty question we ask when nations rage:
Just when will be Christ's coming, the ending of the age?
Take care, said Jesus clearly, for many will appear;
They'll claim to be Messiah, yet people should not fear.

For in the days of Noah, the people went along
In eating and in drinking, in merriment and song—
Then suddenly the world changed with great, surprising
    power;
So too will be Christ's coming, and no one knows the
    hour.

So keep awake and watchful; salvation is at hand!
Our hope is in Christ Jesus, and by God's grace we stand.
The night is almost over, we wait for God's new day,
And through the Holy Spirit, we follow Jesus' way.

Be ready in your living, for when you feed the poor,
Or give to thirsty children the water they long for,
And when you welcome strangers and help the ones in
    need,
Christ says: "Receive my kingdom, for you are serving
    me."

TUNE: Arthur Henry Mann, 1881 ("O Jesus, I Have Promised,"
   LBW 514, NCH 493, PH 388, UMH 396)
TEXT: Copyright © 1998 by Carolyn Winfrey Gillette. All rights
   reserved.

21 God, We Await Your Advent Here

MARYTON   LM

God, we await your advent here:
When will these desert lands rejoice?
When will new blossoms bright appear
And all earth praise you with one voice?

We live in deserts we have made;
Gifts of your love we pass right by.
We seek possessions, more each day,
And then in thirst for joy, we cry.

God, we prepare for Jesus' birth—
Searching for gifts from store to store!
Yet when you sent your Christ to earth,
You gave us joy worth so much more.

When in the love of Christ we grow,
Streams in this desert shall abound.
Then by your Spirit we will know:
True wealth in Jesus Christ is found.

TUNE: Henry Percy Smith, 1874 ("O Master, Let Me Walk with Thee,"
    HY 660, LBW 492, NCH 503, PH 357, UMH 430)
TEXT: Copyright © 1998 by Carolyn Winfrey Gillette. All rights
    reserved.

O God, Our Words Cannot Express

(Tune: ST. ANNE CM "Our God, Our Help in Ages Past")

by Carolyn Winfrey Gillette

O God, our words cannot express
The pain we feel this day.
Enraged, uncertain, we confess
Our need to bow and pray.

We grieve for all who lost their lives...
And for each injured one.
We pray for children, husbands, wives
Whose grief has just begun.

O Lord, we're called to offer prayer
For all our leaders, too.
May they, amid such great despair,
Be wise in all they do.

We trust your mercy and your grace;
In you we will not fear!
May peace and justice now embrace!
Be with your people here!

Carolyn Winfrey Gillette is co-pastor with her husband, Bruce, of First Church in Pitman, N.J., and author of Gifts of Love: New Hymns for Today's Worship *(Geneva Press, 2000). Carolyn holds the copyright to this hymn, written on the afternoon of September 11, but gives permission for anyone to use it in a worship setting. This new hymn has been used in worship services throughout the U.S.A. and overseas, and also was on the BBC and PBS-TV. An old friend of* Monday Morning, *Carolyn's first hymn, "Gifts of Love," appeared in our pages.*

Presbyterian Views on Immigration

by John P. Marcum

"It's déjà vu all over again," as Yogi Berra said. He was probably referring to baseball, but I have immigration in mind. Once more— this time prompted in part by the horrific events of September 11—the United States is debating how wide to open the "Golden Door." Let's look at recent Presbyterian opinion on this ongoing issue, taken from the November 2000 Presbyterian Panel survey.

In general, most Presbyterians favor keeping out some form of a welcome mat for the rest of the world. When asked if they would "vote for a law to stop almost all legal immigration into the United States for the next five years," majorities of members (64 percent), elders (75 percent), pastors (90 percent), and specialized clergy (93 percent) responded *no*. Similarly, while few respondents want "the number of immigrants allowed into the U.S." to be *increased*, only 29 percent of members, 21 percent of elders, 8 percent of pastors, and 11 percent of specialized clergy want that number *decreased*.

But many respondents make a distinction when it

22　In a Feedbox, in a Stable

BEECHER　8.7.8.7 D

In a feedbox, in a stable,
Jesus slept upon the hay;
So, our God, you came among us,
Bringing peace on earth that day.
Beautiful upon the mountain!
Christ, you bring us God's shalom;
May we share your love and justice
In each land and town and home.

In a shelter, poor and homeless,
Sleeps a child upon her bed;
In a basement hides a family,
Bombs exploding overhead.
Jesus, you knew want and hunger;
Your own family fled the sword.
May we see you, may we hear you,
In each one oppressed or poor.

In the church, we seek your presence;
Prince of Peace, you meet us here:
See! A person seeking shelter.
See! Another filled with fear.
See! A world where lives are broken;
Give us strength and help us care,
Till our love for every neighbor
Fills each thought and act and prayer.

TUNE: John Zundel, 1870 ("Love Divine, All Loves Excelling,"
    HY 470, NCH 43, PH 343, UMH 384)
ALTERNATE TUNE: HYFRYDOL ("Alleluia! Sing to Jesus!" HY 460,
    LBW 158, NCH 257, PH 144, UMH 196)

SEASONS, SACRAMENTS, AND CELEBRATIONS

23   What a World of Sound

HYMN TO JOY   8.7.8.7 D

What a world of sound it must have
Been for Jesus, newly-born —
Mother Mary singing songs of
Praise to God that Christmas morn;
Joseph, reaching for the child,
Whispering when the baby fussed;
Songs and whispers bear the promise:
You are truly God-with-us.

Surely there were sounds of women
From that small community,
Stopping by to see the baby,
Offering hospitality;
Lambs were bleating, donkeys braying,
Children playing in the street.
Jesus, close against his mother,
Felt her heart's rejoicing beat.

In that town were shepherds calling;
Workers there were cutting wood;
In the distance, angry shouts and
People begging for their food;
In a doorway, someone weeping,
Saddened by some inner pain —
Jesus, in your incarnation,
Unto each of these you came.

What a world of sound we live in;
Many words we daily hear.
'Mid this world's conflicting voices,
Be for us God's Word so clear.
Help us listen to your story;
Help us hear you when we pray.
In you, Jesus, is our hope: God
Came to us on Christmas Day.

TUNE: Ludwig van Beethoven, 1824 ("Joyful, Joyful, We Adore Thee,"
    HY 376, LBW 551, NCH 4, PH 464, UMH 89)
ALTERNATE TUNE: IN BABILONE ("There's a Wideness in God's
    Mercy," HY 495, LBW 523, NCH 23, PH 298, UMH 325)
TEXT: Copyright © 1998 by Carolyn Winfrey Gillette. All rights
    reserved.

24 God, What a Faith-Filled Mystery

ST. ANNE CM

God, what a faith-filled mystery,
That your own Child once died!
In Christ is true humanity—
your love personified.

In all Christ chose to do and say,
He followed you alone—
Then other people turned away,
For his love judged their own.

Christ died a sacrificial lamb;
He showed your wondrous grace.
Christ paid the debt of human sin,
By suffering in our place.

Our shepherd died, our lives to save
From death and pain and sin.
Christ came to ransom every slave;
Now we are bound to him.

O Christ, we call you God and Lord,
And loving Savior, too.
In you, our lives have been restored;
May we now live for you.

TUNE: Attr. William Croft, 1708 ("Our God, Our Help in Ages Past,"
    HY 680, LBW 320, NCH 25, PH 210, UMH 117)
ALTERNATE TUNE: AMAZING GRACE ("Amazing Grace," HY 671,
    LBW 448, NCH 547, PH 280, UMH 378)
TEXT: Copyright © 1999 by Carolyn Winfrey Gillette. All rights
    reserved.

25 Early on a Sunday

PROMISES   11.11.11.9 with refrain

Early on a Sunday, women went to weep
At the tomb of Jesus, for their pain was deep.
All their hopes were shattered, they had lost their friend,
Till they heard: his death was not the end!

Refrain
Christ is risen!
Shout your alleluias and go share the good news!
Love and serve him,
For God has given life and hope anew.

Death has been defeated, with its pain and strife;
God has opened wide for us eternal life.
God has given Christians that new life to share,
Bringing love and justice everywhere.

Refrain

Every week we celebrate your Easter Day
As we come to worship you, and sing and pray.
We recall the empty tomb and know your grace
And your living presence in this place.

Refrain

TUNE: R. Kelso Carter, 1886 ("Standing on the Promises," UMH 374)
TEXT: Copyright © 1999 by Carolyn Winfrey Gillette. All rights
    reserved.

26   Creator of the Water

LANCASHIRE   7.6.7.6 D

Creator of the water that makes the world so green,
That satisfies the thirsty, and keeps us cool and clean,
We take from your creation this gift we use each day;
You call us now to use it in this most holy way.

As in the time of Noah, the sea engulfed the land,
And through the Red Sea, Moses led Israel 'cross the sand,
And to the Jordan waters, Christ went and was baptized—
Your water has a power: it changes all our lives.

May this your gift of water, long springing from the earth,
Become for all new Christians their fountain of rebirth.
Lord, wash away their sinning, and give them life anew—
Pour out your Spirit on them, that they may follow you.

God, through your gift of water, your family we become;
You take away divisions; in Christ you make us one.
Now send your Spirit on us and give us work to do,
That we may share with others the love we have from you.

TUNE: Henry Thomas Smart, 1835 ("The Day of Resurrection!"
    HY 555, LBW 495, NCH 245, PH 118, UMH 303)
ALTERNATE TUNE: ANGEL'S STORY ("O Jesus, I Have Promised,"
    LBW 514, NCH 493, PH 388, UMH 396)
TEXT: Copyright © 1998 by Carolyn Winfrey Gillette. All rights
    reserved.

27 We Gather at Your Table, Lord

TALLIS' CANON   LM

We gather at your table, Lord:
We humbly lift our hearts to you!
Here all are welcomed, all restored,
And all are given work to do.

We share this meal and we are fed.
Such basic gifts become your sign:
We see you broken in the bread;
We know your love in common wine.

God, pour your Spirit on us all,
And on these gifts that we receive;
For in Christ's presence we recall
His life and death, and so believe.

From north and south, from west and east,
Now reconciled, we gather near;
We taste your kingdom's banquet feast,
So finding strength to serve you here.

TUNE: Thomas Tallis. Adapted from Parker's *Whole Psalter*, c. 1561
("All Praise to Thee, My God, This Night," HY 43, LBW 278,
NCH 100, PH 542, UMH 682)
ALTERNATE TUNE: MARYTON ("O Master, Let Me Walk with
Thee," HY 660, LBW 492, NCH 503, PH 357, UMH 430)
TEXT: Copyright © 1999 by Carolyn Winfrey Gillette. All rights
reserved.

28 God, We Sing and Worship

A Hymn for Confirmation

NICAEA   12.13.12.10

God, we sing and worship, joining friends and neighbors,
Sharing with the ones we love the joy of your good news.
We have heard your gospel through our church's labors,
Through loving lives of those who share our pews.

What a joyful gift to learn the faith of others;
Yet we know the greater joy of faith that is our own.
May we know your love for all your sons and daughters:
We live in you, God, we are not alone.

You have given Jesus, you have sent your Spirit;
You have given water as a sign that we belong.
You have given love and called your church to share it;
Through bread and chalice, you have made us strong.

Now we come before you in the faith you gave us,
In the faith that was your gift when we were all baptized.
Jesus is our Lord! You sent him here to save us!
With grateful hearts, we give you now our lives.

TUNE: John Bacchus Dykes, 1861 ("Holy, Holy, Holy, Lord God
    Almighty!" HY 362, LBW 165, NCH 277, PH 138, UMH 64)
TEXT: Copyright © 1998 by Carolyn Winfrey Gillette. All rights
    reserved.

29 God, in Joy We Gather

A Wedding Hymn

NICAEA   12.13.12.10

God, in joy we gather, giving thanks for marriage,
Witnessing the love between this woman and this man.
We with prayers surround them, asking now your blessing:
Strengthen their love, Lord, by your loving hand.

Christ, you blessed a wedding when you went to Cana;
Through your sacrificial love you show us how to live.
Look upon this couple, deepen their commitments;
As you forgive us, teach them to forgive.

Fill them with your Spirit, give them gifts for living:
Faith, so they will trust you as their strength in all they do,
Hope, for you walk with them in their life together,
Love for each other, love for serving you.

TUNE: John Bacchus Dykes, 1861 ("Holy, Holy, Holy! Lord God
    Almighty!" HY 362, LBW 165, NCH 277, PH 138, UMH 64)
TEXT: Copyright © 1998 by Carolyn Winfrey Gillette. All rights
    reserved.

30 God, We Walk Through Death's Deep Valley

VESPER HYMN 8.7.8.7 D

God, we walk through death's deep valley,
Where such grief and pain abound.
In the midst of so much sorrow,
Where, we ask, can you be found?
Where are hope and reassurance?
Who will take away our fear?
God, we trust your presence with us:
In our sorrow, you are here.

As an ordinary pebble
Tossed upon a quiet pond
Sends out rings of rippling waters,
Moving waters far beyond—
So we touch the lives of others;
We are moved by how they live.
Help us, in our joy, remember;
Help us, in our pain, forgive.

"Do not let your hearts be troubled,"
Jesus said to those he loved.
"There are many dwelling places
In my Father's house above."
Jesus, you have gone before us;
Jesus, you will guide us there.
Lord, we trust your hand to lead us
To the place that you prepare.

We hold on to what you promise:
Earth and heav'n will be made new.
Then your home will be among us;
We will always dwell with you.
There will be no sound of weeping;
You will wipe away each tear.
God, we trust your promise to us:
Now and always, you are here.

TUNE: Attributed to Dimitri S. Bortniansky. As in Stevenson's
    A Selection of Popular National Airs, 1818 ("Now, on Land and
    Sea Descending," PH 545, UMH 685)
ALTERNATE TUNE: CONVERSE ("What a Friend We Have in
    Jesus," LBW 439, NCH 506, PH 403, UMH 526)

31 God, Your Blessings Overflow!

DIX   7.7.7.7.7.7

God, your blessings overflow!
What can we begin to say?
How can we begin to show
All our gratitude this day?
God, we join to worship you,
Giving thanks for all you do.

Thank you for the life you give,
For each friend and family,
For the land in which we live,
For your love that sets us free.
Thank you, God, for daily bread,
And for feasts of joy you spread.

Yet at tables where we share,
Sometimes there is also pain.
There may be an empty chair:
When will we feel whole again?
When our days of grief are long,
Thank you that your love is strong.

So we join in thanks this day,
And your gifts we freely share,
So we follow Christ the Way,
Loving, serving everywhere.
Spirit, may our lives express
All our daily thankfulness.

TUNE: Conrad Kocher, 1838. Abr. William Henry Monk, 1861 ("For
the Beauty of the Earth," HY 288, LBW 561, NCH 28, PH 473,
UMH 92)

32 Our God, We Sing and Celebrate

ELLACOMBE   CMD

Our God, we sing and celebrate! Your grace to us is clear!
For we recall your faithful love for all your people here.
We've worked together, yet we know it's not the things
    we've done,
But you, who give us life and hope in sending us your Son.

Lord Jesus, in this broken world, you teach us how to heal,
And in a world where pride abounds, you call your church
    to kneel.
Amid the hate, we're called to love; amid the fear, to pray.
You call us to live differently; transform us every day!

You give us gifts to be your church; we follow as you call.
Here some are teachers, others preach, to speak your truth
    to all.
Some reach to help the sick and poor, while some are
    called to lead;
Yet by your Spirit, we are one, in word, in prayer, in deed!

How easy to look back and see your graceful, constant care,
And yet we're called to look ahead, to grow, to serve, to
    dare!
What is your will in this new day? God, help us pray and
    search,
For as we seek to walk with you, we are your faithful church.

TUNE: *Gesangbuch der Herzogl. Wirtembergischen Katholischen*
    Hofkapelle, 1784; alt. 1868 ("I Sing the Mighty Power of God,"
    HY 210, LBW 251, NCH 12, PH 288, UMH 203)
TEXT: Copyright © 1999 by Carolyn Winfrey Gillette. All rights
    reserved.

33 For This Land in All Its Wonder

CWM RHONDDA   8.7.8.7.8.7.7.

For this land in all its wonder, for each city, farm, and town,
For each mountain filled with splendor, for each place
    where love is found,
For the freedoms we enjoy here,
God, may thanks to you abound! God, may thanks to you
    abound!

For your peace and love unending, breaking barriers that
    divide,
For the joy of cultures blending as we live here side by side,
God, we thank you and we pray now:
May we all be unified! May we all be unified!

For your hand to lead and guide us, for your work in
    history,
For your vision born inside us of a just society,
God, we thank you and we pray now:
May this vision come to be! May this vision come to be!

May we be a nation seeking ways that are both wise and
    fair,
May our living and our speaking serve your purpose
    everywhere.
May we follow where you lead us;
God, this is our hope and prayer! God, this is our hope
    and prayer!

TUNE: John Hughes, 1907 ("God of Grace and God of Glory," HY 594,
    LBW 415, NCH 436, PH 420, UMH 577)
TEXT: Copyright © 1999 by Carolyn Winfrey Gillette. All rights
    reserved.

SEASONS, SACRAMENTS, AND CELEBRATIONS

34 God, How Many Are a Thousand

AUSTRIAN HYMN   8.7.8.7 D

God, how many are a thousand
Out of all the grains of sand,
And how many are a thousand
Of the stars that you command?
Lord, how awesome is the meaning
Of this new day shining bright,
For we know a thousand years are
As a moment in your sight.

God, we look to your vast heavens;
Constellations seem to dance.
In each atom is your detail,
And you form the smallest plants.
When we look back through the ages,
There we see your hand as well.
Thank you, God, for loving, caring
For this world in which we dwell.

God, in Christ, you showed that caring:
You broke through our time and space.
Christ proclaimed how much you love us,
Showing your redeeming grace.
Jesus healed the ones who suffered;
He endured death's mighty pain.
In your time, you raised our Savior;
With him, life begins again.

Yet, O God, our world still searches,
Longing for the peace you give.
In this age when life is changing,
Teach us, Lord, in whom we live.
Show again Christ's risen presence,
Guide us by your Spirit's power.
May we find the joy you offer,
As we serve you every hour.

God, how joyful are a thousand
When we Christians join to sing!
And how mighty are a thousand
When we share the gifts we bring!
Christ, we seek to work together;
Hand in hand you make us strong.
Spirit, help us in this new time:
Give us joy in work and song.

TUNE: Franz Joseph Haydn, 1797 ("Glorious Things of Thee Are
    Spoken," HY 522, LBW 358, NCH 307, PH 446, UMH 731)
ALTERNATE TUNE: BEECHER ("Love Divine, All Loves Excelling,"
    HY 470, NCH 43, PH 343, UMH 384)
TEXT: Copyright © 1998 by Carolyn Winfrey Gillette. All rights
    reserved.

35 On This Day of Celebration

HYMN TO JOY   8.7.8.7. D

On this day of celebration,
At this time when hopes are new,
God, we gather as your people,
Called to put our trust in you.
You have made the world we live in;
You have worked through history.
In your plan we find our purpose,
In your love, our unity.

Long ago, you sent a Savior
To our world in deep despair.
In your Word made flesh you came, our
Life to know, our sins to bear.
Christ has died and Christ is risen!
At this new year we proclaim:
Yesterday, today, forever—
Jesus Christ is still the same!

Through two thousand years of changes,
Through these passing centuries,
You have called your church to witness
To Christ's love that claims and frees.
Each new generation hears you,
Each must find a fresh new way
To make known the life you offer,
To the people in their day.

On this day, we pause and wonder
What the future years will bring,
Yet we know you clothe each flower
And you make each sparrow sing.
How much more will you protect us
With your guiding, caring hand!
By your Spirit, lead us boldly
In the future you have planned.

TUNE: Ludwig van Beethoven, 1824 ("Joyful, Joyful, We Adore Thee,"
    HY 376, LBW 551, NCH 4, PH 464, UMH 89)
TEXT: Copyright © 1999 by Carolyn Winfrey Gillette. All rights
    reserved.

36 Christ Be with Us

CONVERSE 8.7.8.7 D

Christ be with us, Christ behind us,
Christ before us—all around!
Christ in busy, noisy cities,
Christ where hardly rings a sound.
Jesus, you're our Lord and Savior;
On your love we can depend.
Help us see your presence clearly
In each stranger and each friend.

Christ in lines of people fleeing,
Praying that a war will cease;
Christ in battered women's shelters,
Looking for a place of peace.
Christ with people sick or dying,
Loved ones trying hard to cope—
In this world of so much suffering,
Christ, you give your people hope.

Christ with children who must struggle,
Working hard for daily food;
Christ in classrooms, learning, growing,
Asking questions, seeking good;
Christ in diners, waiting tables;
Christ in homes where children play—
In this world of people working,
Christ, you work through us today.

Christ with all who keep on struggling,
Helping others to be free;
Christ with churches working, searching
For a greater unity;
Christ, in bread and wine, be with us,
Giving strength for each new day—
In this world of daily crosses,
Be our joyful, living Way.

TUNE: Charles Crozat Converse, 1868 ("What a Friend We Have in
    Jesus," LBW 439, NCH 506, PH 403, UMH 526)
ALTERNATE TUNE: HYFRYDOL ("Alleluia, Sing to Jesus," HY 460,
    LBW 158, NCH 257, PH 144, UMH 196)
TEXT: Copyright © 1998 by Carolyn Winfrey Gillette. All rights
    reserved.

37 The Storm Came to Honduras

PASSION CHORALE   7.6.7.6 D

The storm came to Honduras, to Nicaraguan towns;
El Salvador felt anguish as rains came crashing down.
O God of wind and water who made the sea and sky,
Amid such great destruction, we ask a mournful, "Why?"

Great walls of mud and water swept homes and towns
    away:
A thousand Rachels weep now for children lost today,
A million madres mourn now as rivers flood the shore—
O Jesus, friend and Savior, you suffer with the poor.

A weaving loom is shattered, a school in ruin lies,
A bridge is washed down-river, a lonely child cries;
O Spirit, send your comfort—and give us faith that dares.
For when our neighbors suffer, our lives are bound to
    theirs.

TUNE: Hans Leo Hassler, 1601. Harm. Johann Sebastian Bach, 1729
    ("O Sacred Head, Now Wounded," HY 168, LBW 117, NCH 226,
    PH 98, UMH 286)
ALTERNATE TUNE: ANGEL'S STORY ("O Jesus, I Have Promised,"
    LBW 514, NCH 493, PH 388, UMH 396)

38   A Prayer for Our Children

HERZLIEBSTER JESU   11.11.11.5

God, we have heard it, sounding in the silence:
News of the children lost to this world's violence.
Children of promise! Then without a warning,
Loved ones are mourning.

Jesus, you came to bear our human sorrow;
You came to give us hope for each tomorrow.
You are our life, Lord—God's own love revealing.
We need your healing!

Heal us from giving weapons any glory;
Help us, O Prince of Peace, to hear your story;
Help us resist the evil all around here;
May love abound here!

By your own Spirit, give your church a clear voice;
In this world's violence, help us make a new choice.
Help us to witness to the joy your peace brings,
Until your world sings!

TUNE: Johann Crüger, 1640 ("Ah, Holy Jesus," HY 158, LBW 123,
    NCH 218, PH 93, UMH 289)
TEXT: Copyright © 1999 by Carolyn Winfrey Gillette. All rights
    reserved.

39 God, Your Gift of Peace Is Precious

CWM RHONDDA   8.7.8.7.8.7.7.

God, your gift of peace is precious
In this world of sin and loss:
You have given joy and gladness,
Making peace through Jesus' cross.
God, in love you came to save us,
Giving freedom from our sin—
In you, gifts of peace begin.

Jesus, you are God's example
In the life on earth you lived.
Help us see your face in others,
Teach us freely to forgive.
When, in all your children's conflicts,
Hate and violence increase—
Blest are those who work for peace.

Blessed are the poor in spirit;
Blessed, too, are all the meek.
When we feel a slap of hatred,
You say: Turn the other cheek.
When arrested in the garden
You spoke to your friend to say,
"Peter, put your sword away."

Spirit, help us work for justice
In each challenge that we face.
Each one needs to have the other:
Righteousness and peace embrace.
Children hungry? People homeless?
Missiles flying through the air?
You seek peace with justice there.

So we pray and work together
Toward a world of your shalom.
May all people share your bounty,
And all have both feast and home.
Wolf and lamb shall feed together:
In your kingdom war shall cease,
And your people live in peace.

TUNE: John Hughes, 1907 ("God of Grace and God of Glory," HY 594,
    LBW 415, NCH 436, PH 420, UMH 577)
TEXT: Copyright © 1998 by Carolyn Winfrey Gillette. All rights
    reserved.

40   When Did We See You Hungry, Lord?

A Hymn Dialogue for Congregation and Soloist (or Choir)

MARYTON   LM

Congregation: When did we see you hungry, Lord?
Solo: "I work two jobs so we can eat—
I search for food we can afford—
I am your neighbor down the street!"

Congregation: When did we see you thirsty, Lord?
Solo: "I carry water miles each day—
I long for water, close and pure—
I am your neighbor far away!"

Congregation: When were you still a stranger, Lord?
Solo: "I moved to your community—
I wait your hand at your church door—
I am each stranger that you see!"

Congregation: We see the child whose shoes are worn,
We see the man in hospice care,
We see the prisoner many scorn.
A voice cries out; will we be there?

Jesus, your presence here is real;
You came, a servant on your knees.
May we, your church, now humbly kneel
And serve you in "the least of these."

TUNE: Henry Percy Smith, 1874 ("O Master, Let Me Walk with Thee,"
HY 660, LBW 492, NCH 503, PH 357, UMH 430)
TEXT: Copyright © 1998 by Carolyn Winfrey Gillette. All rights
reserved.

THE CHURCH IN THE WORLD

41   What a Joy, This Habitation!

HYMN TO JOY   8.7.8.7 D

What a joy, this Habitation!
What a day to celebrate!
God, you built the firm foundation
For this home we dedicate.
As our refuge and our shelter,
You surround us with your care;
You have given hands for building,
Hearts for caring, love to share.

Jesus, we have worked together;
Side by side you've made us strong;
In both sun and stormy weather,
You have filled our work with song.
Master builder, you are with us,
Guiding us in all we do;
As we work to build new houses,
So you build our lives anew.

By your Spirit's loving presence,
Bless this home and family here.
Bless the labor all have offered;
Bless each willing volunteer.
Help us as we keep on working
Toward the day when there shall be
Homes and wholeness, peace and justice,
For your whole community.

MUSIC: Ludwig van Beethoven, 1824 ("Joyful, Joyful, We Adore Thee,"
    HY 376, LBW 551, NCH 4, PH 464, UMH 89)
ALTERNATE TUNE: IN BABILONE ("There's a Wideness in God's
    Mercy," HY 495, LBW 523, NCH 23, PH 298, UMH 325)
TEXT: Copyright © 1999 by Carolyn Winfrey Gillette. All rights
    reserved.

THE CHURCH IN THE WORLD

42 God, You Love the World!

A Hymn of Dedication Before a
Mission Trip/Closing Hymn

ARGENTINA   11.11.11.11 with refrain

God, you love the world! You sent your only Son,
And you said, "Go share my love with everyone."
So we seek to serve you in our homes and towns,
And we work to show the world: Your love abounds!

> *Refrain*
> Lead us, as we go this day;
> Guide us as we work and pray.
> Give us, when each day is through,
> True joy, found in serving you.

By your Spirit, some build houses, safe and strong,
Some are called to share your Word in prayer and song.
Some are called to heal the sick and fight disease,
Some are called to save the land by planting trees.

> *Refrain*

Teach us that in loving, we must listen well.
Help us hear the stories others have to tell.
Help us learn from other people and their ways.
May we be united as we offer praise.

> *Refrain*

TUNE: Argentine folk melody ("Song of Hope," PH 432)
TEXT: Copyright © 1999 by Carolyn Winfrey Gillette. All rights
   reserved.

43 Come, You Hungry Ones

KUM BA YAH   8.8.8.5

"Come, you hungry ones," Jesus said.
"Come to me and know: I am Bread!
Come, you weary ones; you are blest!
In me, find your rest."

Hear our cry, O God, hear our prayer!
Heal the ones who know deep despair;
Mend the broken ones from their pain.
Make them whole again.

God, we need you, too, so we pray:
Give us life and health every day.
Give us joy and peace, trusting you.
In Christ, make us new.

We are saved, O Lord, by your grace;
We are healed and sent from this place.
Through your Spirit's gifts, may we share
Your love everywhere.

TUNE: African melody ("Kum ba Yah," PH 338, UMH 494)
TEXT: Copyright © 1999 by Carolyn Winfrey Gillette. All rights
    reserved.

44 God, How Can We Comprehend?

ABERYSTWYTH 7.7.7.7. D

God, how can we comprehend—
Though we've seen them times before—
Lines of people without end,
Fleeing from some senseless war?
They seek safety anywhere,
Hoping for a welcome hand!
Can we know the pain they bear?
Can we ever understand?

You put music in their souls;
Now they struggle to survive.
You gave each one gifts and goals;
Now they flee to stay alive.
God of outcasts, may we see
How you value everyone,
For each homeless refugee
Is your daughter or your son.

Lord, your loving knows no bounds;
You have conquered death for all.
May we hear beyond our towns
To our distant neighbors' call.
Spirit, may our love increase;
May we reach to all your earth,
Till each person lives in peace;
Till your world sees each one's worth.

TUNE: Joseph Parry, 1879 ("Watchman, Tell Us of the Night," HY 699,
LBW 91, NCH 103, PH 303, UMH 479)

TEXT: Copyright © 1999 by Carolyn Winfrey Gillette. All rights
reserved.

45 God, You Wrap Your Love Around Us

CONVERSE   8.7.8.7. D

God, you wrap your love around us,
Like a blanket, soft and warm.
You give rest when we are weary,
You protect us from the storm.
May each person who finds shelter
In these blankets that we share
Also feel the joy and comfort
Of your love's protecting care.

Jesus, you were once a baby,
Sought by those who would destroy.
Into Egypt you were carried—
Far from home, a little boy.
Were you wrapped up warm to travel,
Safe from terror, free from harm?
Did you feel God's strong protection,
Snuggled there in Mary's arm?

May the women, men, and children
Fleeing danger every day
Know, through us, your living presence;
You walk with them on their way.
Spirit, as you give them comfort,
Teach us here to freely give;
May we blanket this world over
With your love, so all may live.

TUNE: Charles Crozat Converse, 1868 ("What a Friend We Have in
    Jesus," LBW 439, NCH 506, PH 403, UMH 526)

ALTERNATE TUNE: BEECHER ("Love Divine, All Loves Excelling,"
HY 470, NCH 43, PH 343, UMH 384)

Commentary
on the Hymns

The following paragraphs are designed to be used or adapted for use as hymn notes in church worship bulletins. Scripture quotations are from the New Revised Standard Version of the Bible. For some of the scripture passages that inspired the hymns, see the Index of Biblical References.

THE BIBLE: SINGING THE STORY

1 Your Word Is Like a Lamp, O Lord

This hymn is based on Psalm 119:105: "Your word is a lamp to my feet and a light to my path." Christians continue to find the benefits of daily Bible reading for their spiritual growth. They are also discovering that the Bible is, as the Presbyterian Church's *Confession of 1967* describes it, a "witness without parallel" in telling God's wonderful deeds (*Book of Confessions*, 9.27). As we read the Bible, it is essential to approach it with "literary and historical understanding" (9.29). Yet while cultures change, the good news of God's gracious love is unchanging. The last verse of the hymn is a prayer for illumination, asking God to help us understand and respond to the good news we have read and heard.

2 God Made the Heavens and the Earth

A theologian once commented that Christians sometimes forget that the first act of God's grace is not what God did in Jesus Christ, but what God did in creation. This hymn follows the account of creation in Genesis 1 and in Psalm 8, a psalm celebrating creation. God made us stewards, or caretakers, of this wonderful world; the refrain reminds us of our human responsibility to care for all that God has made. More and more, the church needs to see environmental issues as issues of faithfulness and Christian stewardship. This hymn was posted on the National Council of Churches' Web site dealing with environmental issues and has been used for Earth Day Sunday celebrations.

3 Long Ago, God Reached in Love

Martha Bettis Gee, an editor of the new Presbyterian curriculum *Covenant People*, expressed interest in having a hymn for children with a covenant theme. This hymn uses several of the Old Testament common lectionary texts for the Lenten season, year B: God's covenant with Noah, God's covenant with Abraham and Sarah; the giving of the law at Sinai, the new covenant shown to Jeremiah, and the new covenant fulfilled in the life, death, and resurrection of Jesus Christ. The refrain, emphasizing that God is faithful, ends with "your covenant is love," a reminder of the Hebrew concept of *hesed*, God's steadfast love.

4 Spirit of God

When many Christians think of the Holy Spirit, we tend to think of Pentecost. Yet throughout the scriptures we can see the Spirit of God at work in many wonderful ways. The Hebrew word *ruach* and the Greek word *pneuma* have three meanings, all of which are included in this hymn: breath, wind, and spirit. The hymn picks up on the idea from the Nicene Creed that the Holy Spirit is "the Lord, the giver of life," and on the idea, found in the Presbyterian Church (U.S.A.)'s *Brief Statement of Faith*, that the Holy Spirit gives us courage.

5 God of the Women

This hymn mentions specific women in the Bible and faithful women of today. The first verse's use of "trusting" parallels that of the Presbyterian *Brief Statement of Faith*, which uses "trust" instead of "believe" as it describes examples of faithfulness found in Sarah, Hannah, and Ruth. The second verse's reference to "Way" is one of the earliest descriptions of Christians (Acts 9:2). "Mary, Joanna, Susanna, and more" comes from the story in Luke 8:1–3, a story of women who supported Jesus with their financial resources. "Learning to pray" is a reminder that Jesus taught women as well as men, going against some customs of his day. The third verse recalls the painful history for women of faith. "Left out of stories" refers to the way in which biblical writers often ignore women (for example, Matt. 14:21 tells that Jesus fed "five thousand men, not counting the women and children"). These slights are minor compared to what Phyllis Trible has written about in her *Texts of Terror*—biblical stories like 2 Samuel 13:1–22 and Judges 11:29–40; 19:1–30. The reference to the smiling at a girl's birth is a positive one, yet too few of the biblical stories celebrate girls' arrivals or list many women in genealogies. The fourth verse begins with the Easter story where women were the first witnesses to the resurrection. Acts 1:14 tells us that women joined the other followers before Pentecost and also were empowered by the Holy Spirit (Acts 2:1–21). The fifth verse refers to Phoebe. Paul's personal greetings in his letter to the Romans include this statement: "I have good things to say about Phoebe, who is a leader in the church . . . she has proved to be a respected leader for many others, including me" (Rom. 16:1–2, CEV). The footnote in the NRSV Bible says the position that Phoebe held can be translated "minister," as it is in the one other place the Greek word appears—when it describes a man (Eph. 6:21). "Ministers all" relates well to the Presbyterian Church's *Brief Statement of Faith*, which affirms that "The same Spirit who inspired the prophets and apostles . . . calls women and men to all ministries of the Church." This hymn was published in *The Presbyterian Outlook* as well as in the national Episcopal women's magazine *Communique* and has been translated into Japanese by a Roman Catholic group for publication in Japan. It has been used on Mother's Day and on Sundays celebrating the gifts of women in the church.

6 Gifts of Love

"Gifts of Love" was the first hymn written by Carolyn Winfrey Gillette. During the summer of 1998, she attended the Synod of the Trinity's Synod School at Wilson College (a Presbyterian-related college in Chambersburg, Pennsylvania). A teacher in a class on the Psalms mentioned that people often remember things set to music and that someone had once written the Ten Commandments as a hymn, but no one knew that hymn. Carolyn decided to write one to help her three young children, John, Catherine, and Sarah, learn the Ten Commandments. The hymn's title comes from our understanding that God gave us the commandments out of great love (see Ps. 119). The music for this hymn, usually associated with "Lord, I Want to Be a Christian," has a prayerful quality that reminds us how much we need God's help to keep these commandments. The hymn was first sung by vacation Bible school children at the First Presbyterian Church in Cape May, New Jersey, in 1998. Their pastor, Kathy Stoner-LaSala, reported that they particularly liked singing to their parents the words "Listen here! Listen well!"

7 Sing Out! Sound the Trumpets! Proclaim Jubilee!

This hymn was inspired by the theme for the Presbyterian Women's Churchwide Gathering in 2000. It was sung at a national meeting of the American Baptist Churches in the U.S.A. in 1999. Luke 4:16–21 is the account of Jesus beginning his ministry, where he quoted from the book of Isaiah; the refrain of the hymn is a paraphrase of this quote. The hymn acknowledges that, in too many ways, our world has not experienced the freeing gift of love in Jesus Christ. God calls the church to continue Christ's ministry in our troubled world today. The tune TO GOD BE THE GLORY is a triumphant one that expresses confidence and hope that God's kingdom will be realized, by God's grace.

8 Blessed Are the Poor Among You

The Beatitudes turn our understanding of the world upside down. They go against everything that we tend to take for granted: that the rich, the successful, the powerful, and the ones who have not experienced loss are the happy ones. Instead, Jesus tells us, "Blessed are you who are poor. Blessed are you who are hungry now. Blessed are you who weep now." As Thomas G. Long points out in his commentary on Matthew, many of the Beatitudes are in the present tense, while the reasons people are blessed are in the future tense. We live as Christians with two realities—what is, and what is to come. Luke's version of the Beatitudes is less well known than Matthew's version, in part because it immediately follows the blessings with warnings. In both versions, we are told that God is working in unexpected ways to bring about the kingdom. When we allow God to turn our lives around, we find true joy.

9 In Cana at a Wedding Feast

There are few hymns in most hymnals about Jesus' miracles, in spite of the fact that there are numerous biblical stories of Jesus doing these extraordinary deeds. This hymn does not seek to explain the miracles, but celebrates them as pointing beyond themselves to the one who does these "deeds of power, deeds of love." Miracles of nature (including the only miracle found in all four Gospels, the feeding of the five thousand men plus women and children) and miracles of healing are remembered, as they can still speak to us today.

10 God's Great Love Is So Amazing!

This hymn is based on the three "lost and found" parables of Jesus in Luke 15. We need to remember that Jesus' teachings were always in the context of what was happening in his life and ministry. Jesus told these three stories in response to some religious leaders who were grumbling about the kinds of people who were trying to follow him. The hymn seeks to express, as the parables do, God's joy when the lost ones are found. The final line of each stanza is a reminder of the implications of these parables for the church and for individual Christians today. We need to ask ourselves: What does it mean for us that God welcomes all kinds of people into the church? What does our relationship with God's "other" children need to be? How can we share in God's joy?

11 When You Are Praying

The Lord's Prayer is found in the larger context of Jesus' teaching on prayer in the Sermon on the Mount. The first and last verses of this hymn provide the context; the second, third, and fourth verses paraphrase the Lord's Prayer itself. The tune AMAZING GRACE is a reminder of the wonderful, gracious gift that prayer is for Christians.

12 *Mary Heard the Angel's Message*

This hymn was written as a gift for Carolyn's father-in-law, Gerald Gillette, who is a Roman Catholic. Protestants often under-emphasize the important role of Mary, maybe in part due to a perceived overemphasis in other traditions. This hymn seeks to celebrate the biblical story of Mary and her faithfulness that has led some to describe her as "the first disciple."

THE CHURCH: GOD'S LOVING COMMUNITY

13 *I Believe*

The Apostles' Creed, the Ten Commandments, and the Lord's Prayer are often used together to teach the basics of the Christian faith. Tom Hastings, a professor at Union Seminary in Tokyo, suggested this hymn paraphrasing the Apostles' Creed, as part of a set of three hymns on these foundational statements. This "creed of generations" has spoken to the Christian church for centuries and continues to speak to the church today. Many churches use the creed every Sunday; this hymn offers a new way to affirm our faith.

14 *Our God, We Are a Church Reformed*

Many churches celebrate the last Sunday in October as Reformation Sunday. This hymn begins by acknowledging that God calls all churches to be "reformed and reforming" as they seek to follow God in a changing world. The second through fifth verses lift up key points of "Faith in the Reformed Tradition" found in the end of the second chapter of the Presbyterian *Book of Order* (G-2.0500). The hymn also lifts up the theme of God's sacrificial love in Jesus Christ as a helpful correction to an overemphasis on the sovereignty of God (as suggested in Shirley Guthrie's *Christian Doctrine*, Westminster John Knox Press, 1994, p. 103). William Chapman uses this hymn in his book *History and Theology in the Book of Order* (Witherspoon Press, 1999).

15 Welcoming God

In his life, teaching, and ministry, Jesus sought to include people who were often excluded by others. Jesus blessed the children, included women among his followers, had table fellowship with sinners and outcasts, and proclaimed God's good news to people who were poor. So the Gospels remind us that Christ calls the church to be a community that welcomes all people in his name. This hymn seeks to remind us that when we welcome others, we welcome Jesus.

16 God of Generations

This hymn celebrates the many ways that God calls people of all ages to carry out the church's work. Reflecting the words of Psalm 148 and how all are called to praise God, "Young men and women alike, old and young together" (v. 12), it lifts up biblical examples of children, youth, and adults, to remind us that God gives gifts to all, for the building up of the church and the carrying out of its ministry. Many times church members have said that "children are the future of the church," but it is just as true that they can do real ministry right now. In the same way, God chooses to work through youth, and through middle-aged and older adults. Many churches find that the tune NICAEA is a popular one for Christians of all ages.

17 Hear My Prayer for Unity

Many people know the prayer that Jesus taught his disciples, found in the Sermon on the Mount, but his prayer in John 17 is less well known. We live in a time when churches struggle with many issues that divide us. We are divided from other churches, and we are divided within congregations. This hymn begins with Jesus' prayer for the church, and continues with our prayer, that we may be united so the world may know God's love for all, through our unified witness.

18 We Thank You, God, for Teachers

This hymn, written to be used on a Christian Education Sunday, is a prayer of thanksgiving for all who help us grow in our faith.

Our churches are strengthened by good church school teachers who teach by loving example as well as by words; they are also strengthened by willing learners of all ages, by families who teach children in their homes what it means to live out their faith, and by all of our members who nurture and support each other. Thanks be to God for all who teach and learn and help others grow as Christians.

19 O God, in Your Love

Churches are enriched by the wonderful diversity of people whom God has called together for mission and ministry. Too often, groups of people feel excluded from the community of God's people, and from participating in the church's ministry. Freda Gardner, retired professor of Christian Education at Princeton Seminary and Moderator of the 1999 Presbyterian General Assembly, has said it well: "When we know that it is God who gives gifts to us, why do we have a hard time believing that the gifts are given for the common good? The gifts of God are for all the people of God." This hymn is a prayer that our common faith in Jesus Christ and our willingness to serve him will overcome the things that divide us, and will unite us in mission and ministry.

SEASONS, SACRAMENTS, AND CELEBRATIONS

20 There Is a Mighty Question

The first Sunday of Advent begins a new year in the Christian calendar. This first Sunday celebrates the coming of Christ not in the past, on Christmas, but in the future. While our churches confess with the Apostles' Creed that Christ "will come again to judge the living and the dead," we often err on one side or another. Some churches never talk about Christ's coming in the future, and others seem to talk of nothing else. This hymn seeks to take seriously the biblical teaching about Jesus' coming, including where Jesus says that "about that day and hour no one knows" (Matt. 24:36). While we may not know God's time line, we do have the gift of hope that God's will is going to be accomplished. The hymn reminds us that we are called to be obedient as we seek to "follow Jesus' way" today.

21 God, We Await Your Advent Here

United States culture is one that too often encourages us to seek immediate gratification and to look for happiness in material abundance. Our faith often involves times of waiting upon God. True joy cannot be found in possessions alone. Augustine's famous prayer states that "our hearts are restless until they rest in you." This hymn invites us to look for our Christmas joy in Jesus Christ, the one whose birth we prepare to celebrate. It first appeared on the front cover of a December 1998 issue of *The Presbyterian Outlook*.

22 In a Feedbox, in a Stable

The biblical Christmas story clearly tells us that the one we worship as Lord came into the world in very humble surroundings. Luke 2:24, with its reference to Leviticus 12:8, shows that Jesus' parents were poor. Jesus' mother could only offer the sacrifice of a poor woman, after Jesus was born. Matthew's account of Jesus' birth describes how his parents fled with him into Egypt some time after his birth. The church needs to be continually concerned for all who are hungry, poor, and oppressed.

23 What a World of Sound

The writer of this hymn is the mother of three young children. Her favorite Christmas carol is "Silent Night," yet any parent of young children may occasionally wonder if a home with a new baby or a young child can be silent for too long. This hymn celebrates the sounds that Jesus might have heard as an infant. We imagine Mary singing to her new baby, the often-forgotten Joseph caring for him, joyful sounds of children playing nearby and women visiting, as well as the more troubling sounds of people who are suffering. This hymn reminds us that Jesus came for all these people. The true joy of Christmas is seen in the context of a hurting world that needs to hear God's good news in Jesus Christ. Beethoven's tune HYMN TO JOY conveys the joy of the day for all Christians.

24 God, What a Faith-Filled Mystery

A variety of biblical images help us understand the meaning of the atonement. These are summarized in the Presbyterian Church's *Confession of 1967*: "God's reconciling act in Jesus Christ is a mystery. . . . It is called the sacrifice of a lamb, a shepherd's life given for his sheep, atonement by a priest; again it is the ransom of a slave, payment of debt, vicarious satisfaction of a legal penalty, and victory over the powers of evil" (9.09). This Good Friday hymn lifts up many of these images as we ponder the meaning of Christ's loving sacrifice for us.

25 Early on a Sunday

The church worships on the first day of the week because in this way we celebrate the day of Jesus' resurrection. The Ten Commandments call for God's people to worship and rest on the seventh day in thankfulness for the gift of creation. Christians worship on the first day because we are a new creation, because what God did in Jesus Christ on that first Easter long ago brings us "life and hope anew" today. This Easter hymn begins with the grief of Good Friday and quickly moves to the joyous news that Christ is risen. We are called to love him and serve him in gratitude. The final verse reminds Christians of the importance of corporate worship, for as a gathered, worshiping community we hear God's story, experience God's grace, and know God's living presence.

26 Creator of the Water

This hymn lifts up images of the common uses for water (drinking, washing, etc.), to remind us how God uses the ordinary to do extra-ordinary (sacramental) things in our world. The hymn uses many of the biblical images found in the 1993 Presbyterian *Book of Common Worship*'s baptismal prayer (see pages 410–11). The biblical stories of salvation are connected with our stories here and now. By the Holy Spirit in baptism we are given faith, made a part of the church and sent out in loving service in God's world. The tune for this hymn, originally associated with the Easter hymn "The Day of Resurrection," reminds us that baptism is the beginning of our new life in our risen Lord. The Pitman, New Jersey, Presbyterian congregation sang it for the first time at the baptism of Seth Alward MacLaughlin.

27 We Gather at Your Table, Lord

This hymn parallels the eucharistic prayer beginning with the *Sursum Corda*, the lifting up of our hearts to God. If you look up the word "heart" in a Bible dictionary you will see that in the scriptures this word "heart" represents the whole of one's being. The second verse of the hymn states that God uses the ordinary to remind us of extra-ordinary things. The bread and the wine are visible signs of God's love. We ask for the presence of God's Spirit in the part of the eucharistic prayer called the epiclesis, which is found in the third verse of the hymn, along with our understanding that Christ is uniquely present for us in this sacrament. The hymn concludes with the image that this meal is a unifying one and a foretaste of the heavenly meal we all will share. It gives us strength to serve God here and now, even as we wait for a new heaven and a new earth.

28 God, We Sing and Worship

This hymn was originally written for two people. Carol A. Krause, then pastor of the Congregational United Church of Christ, New Hampton, Iowa, was an early supporter of Carolyn's hymnwriting. When Tina Rosonke and Jonas Schwickerath were to be confirmed at this church, they looked for a new hymn that would be appropriate for confirmation. It was first sung there on November 1, 1998. The truth of the old African proverb that it takes a whole village to raise a child can be applied to the Christian faith—it takes a whole church to nurture a Christian. The hymn celebrates how a church teaches in the pews and classrooms, and through members' daily living. Confirmation is related to baptism with the line "You have given water as a sign that we belong." This image of belonging, an important one for teens, can also be found in the words of the first question of the *Heidelberg Catechism* that has an authoritative role for the United Church of Christ and Presbyterians: "What is your only comfort, in life and in death?" "That I belong—body and soul, in life and in death—not to myself but to my faithful Savior, Jesus Christ." The 1991 *Brief Statement of Faith* of the

Presbyterian Church (U.S.A.) begins with similar wording: "In life and in death we belong to God . . . whom alone we worship and serve." This faith of the church is reaffirmed in this hymn. John Bacchus Dykes's tune NICAEA is best associated with the hymn titled "Holy, Holy, Holy, Lord God Almighty!" which is popular with all ages.

29 God, in Joy We Gather

There are few wedding hymns in most hymnals. This one is written to a popular tune most commonly associated with "Holy, Holy, Holy, Lord God Almighty!" It serves as a prayer of blessing to be offered by the family and friends gathered for a wedding. The design of the hymn is trinitarian, and the final verse includes a reference to 1 Corinthians 13, the well-known chapter on love, with a prayer that the couple may have God's gifts of faith, hope, and love in their marriage.

30 God, We Walk Through Death's Deep Valley

The most beloved chapter of the Bible, the Twenty-third Psalm, is the source for the first verse of this hymn, which can be used at funerals and on other occasions. As we face the deep valleys of our lives, we know that God is with us, even in times of fear and sorrow. The second verse uses an image from nature to acknowledge how our lives can touch other lives, and how our memories from the past can be a source of comfort. John 14 and Revelation 21 provide the basis for the final two verses, which remind us that our ultimate comfort can be found in God's eternal love. The hymn concludes with the vision, from the last book of the Bible, of a time and place where suffering, tears, and death will be no more.

31 God, Your Blessings Overflow

George Herbert has a wonderful prayer: "Thou hast given so much to me; give one thing more—a grateful heart." This Thanksgiving hymn reminds us in days of joyful celebration that all that we have comes from God alone. It also acknowledges that, even in times of great joy, there can be grief because loved ones are no longer with us. In the end, we are called to live out our gratitude as Christians by giving freely to others, and by loving and serving those in need.

32 Our God, We Sing and Celebrate

This hymn celebrating a church anniversary is based on the 12th chapter of Paul's letter to the church in Rome. It reminds us of the variety of gifts God has given to the church, and of the unity we are given by the Holy Spirit who draws us together as one. Whenever a church celebrates an anniversary, it looks to the past, yet it also looks to the future. "What is your will in this new day?" becomes our prayer to God as we seek to be a faithful church.

33 For This Land in All Its Wonder

This hymn was written to be used at times of national celebration. It celebrates the gifts of God's creation that are evident in the land around us in many ways. Yet many of God's blessings are of a different kind. We see God's presence in history and God's gifts of love and peace that bring us together as a people. God calls us to respond to these gifts, by working together for the justice that God desires.

34 God, How Many Are a Thousand

This hymn draws inspiration from Christians' reflections on 2,000 years of Christian history. A period of one thousand, or two thousand, years seems like an incredible span of time for us, yet we are reminded that these years are just a "moment in God's sight." While the vastness of God's time and God's power seem overwhelming at times, we also believe that the Creator of this vast universe chose to enter our world at a specific time in human history in Jesus, to suffer and die and be raised from death, all out of love for us. We joyfully affirm that God's Spirit continues to empower the church as we face the unique challenges of the new time that is ahead.

35 On This Day of Celebration

This hymn was commissioned by the Rev. John Ash for the Millennium Ecumenical Service on January 1, 2000, in Mays Landing, New Jersey, and was published in a January 2000 issue of *The Presbyterian Outlook*. The hymn may be used at any New Year's celebration or other anniversary celebration as it includes the themes of God's sovereignty, abiding presence, and promise for the future.

THE CHURCH IN THE WORLD

36 Christ Be with Us

This hymn begins with some words from the Breastplate of St. Patrick (389–461) that celebrate Christ's presence in our world. It asks God to "help us see your presence clearly, in each stranger and each friend." The hymn lifts up images of Christ among refugees, with victims of domestic abuse, and with people facing the universal experiences of illness, suffering, and death—all of whom are yearning for hope. The images of Christ present in daily work make the hymn a good one for Labor Day Sunday. *The Presbyterian Outlook* published it with the suggestion that it be used on World Communion Sunday, because it lifts up global concerns and includes themes of Christian unity and the Lord's Supper. The tune, used originally with the hymn "What a Friend We Have in Jesus," reminds us that throughout the difficult times in our lives, Christ is present with us, especially in times of suffering.

37 The Storm Came to Honduras

In the fall of 1998, a powerful hurricane pounded several countries in Central America. In Honduras, thousands of people were killed in the floods that were so much a part of this storm. This hymn, which is trinitarian in form, asks God the question, "Why?" We know that much of the devastation in Honduras and other countries was the result of poverty; for example, the poor often have no safe places to build homes, and the land is deforested as people search for firewood, leading to erosion and flooding. As Christians, we believe that Jesus cries with the poor in their suffering; we are also reminded of God's call to us, to dare to seek changes for a more just and caring world. Truly, "when our neighbors suffer, our lives are bound to theirs."

38 A Prayer for Our Children

This hymn, written during the evening news reports after the 1999 Columbine High School shootings in Colorado, is a prayer for all children, families, and communities who suffer because of violence. It is a lament for children who suffer from school shootings, for children killed in their homes and neighborhoods by guns, and for children lost to violence in war-torn countries far away. It is a prayer for Christians to look seriously at our violence-prone society and to dare to find ways to change, in the name of Jesus Christ, our Prince of Peace.

39 God, Your Gift of Peace Is Precious

Images of peace and justice are abundant throughout the scriptures, and this hymn brings together many of these images. Colossians 1:20–22 tells us that all peacemaking starts with God, who reached out to bring us peace through Jesus Christ. Jesus clearly taught his followers to live in ways of forgiveness, humility, and peace. Psalm 85:10 reminds us that "righteousness and peace will kiss each other"; peace and justice belong together. God calls us to work for a world expressed in the vision of Isaiah 65:21–25, where God's shalom will be for all people.

40 When Did We See You Hungry, Lord?

In Jesus' teaching about the judgment of the nations, the people ask the Son of Man, "Lord, when was it that we saw you hungry and gave you food, or thirsty and gave you something to drink?"(Matt. 25:37–39). This hymn is intended to be sung as a conversation between the congregation and a soloist or choir. When we reach out to the hungry, the thirsty, the stranger, the naked, the sick, and the prisoner, Jesus says we are ministering to him.

41 What a Joy, This Habitation!

This hymn was written at the request of Gloucester County, New Jersey, Habitat for Humanity volunteers who wanted a new hymn to help them celebrate a "Habitation," the dedication of a new home. The volunteers themselves, who come from a number of different denominations, selected the tune as a joyful one that is known in many Christian churches. Whenever we seek to do the work of Jesus Christ in the world, it is important to remember that the work is really God's work. God gives us the talents and the strength and the vision for all we do.

42 God, You Love the World!

This is a hymn of dedication for a mission trip; it may also be used as a hymn of dedication at the close of worship, to celebrate the diversity of gifts that God gives to the church. As Christians, we seek to share the love of God in Jesus Christ with others, using a great variety of talents. It is especially important that we go out into God's world in a spirit of openness to the gifts that others bring. When we respect other people and their unique gifts, when we truly listen to their concerns, we are better able to share in ministry together. The tune ARGENTINA, which is found in *The Presbyterian Hymnal,* is not familiar to everyone; however, it is a joyful and very singable tune that is worth the effort to learn.

43 Come, You Hungry Ones

This hymn lifts up the theme of God's healing in our lives and in the lives of others. It begins with the promises of Jesus: "I am the bread of life. Whoever comes to me will never be hungry, and whoever believes in me will never be thirsty" (John 6:35). "Come to me, all you that are weary and are carrying heavy burdens, and I will give you rest" (Matt. 11:28). The hymn continues as a prayer for healing. It has been used in hospital settings, in Clinical Pastoral Education classes, and in services of wholeness in local churches.

44 God, How Can We Comprehend?

This hymn was written in response to the millions of refugees who have fled their homes as the result of human-made disasters. The insane wars and social injustices that cause people to leave their homes are all too evident in our troubled world. The hymn seeks to recall the precious worth of each person. It speaks of their numerous losses as refugees and asks that we not only see their suffering but respond to their cries for help. Church World Service posted the hymn on its Web site after the tragedy affecting thousands in East Timor.

45 God, You Wrap Your Love Around Us

This hymn was written for congregational celebrations of Church World Service's "Blanket Sunday." The small gift of five dollars will pay for a heavy blanket that can be used by refugees and others in numerous ways—to carry one's possessions or as a small tent, a coat, or warm bedding.

Index of Biblical References

Matthew (continued)

Mark

John (continued)

Acts

Romans

1 Corinthians

Index of Tunes

Metrical Index

Topical Index

Thanksgiving

Wedding

Wholeness and Healing, Service of

Women

Index of First Lines
and Titles